Haruna's Story Part 3

I Talk You Talk Press

CONTENTS

This is Part 3 of Haruna's Story. The story starts in *Haruna's Story Part 1*.

In the story, there are some Japanese words.
The Japanese words are
1. *shacho* - Company President/CEO
2. *san* - Mr/Ms (E.g. Tanaka san = Mr Tanaka)
3. *Izumo* - a city in Japan
4. *Matsue* - a city in Japan
5. *Shimane* - a prefecture in Japan
6. *Izumo Taisha* - a famous shrine in Japan
7. *Golden Week* - A week-long holiday in Japan in May
8. *go-en* - fate / karma / special relationship / special bond to a person
9. *guzen* - a coincidence

CHAPTER ONE

Grace Lily comes to Haruna's shop with her two bodyguards and an assistant. There are many photographers outside the shop. They are taking photographs. Some are trying to get into the shop. A bodyguard stands near the door to stop the photographers entering the shop.

Haruna can see some TV cameras outside. It is very noisy.

"Good morning, Ms Lily," says Haruna. "How are you today?"

"I'm good thank you," says Grace. "Haruna, are you busy?"

"Busy? Er…yes, but…well, er… I work in this shop every day," says Haruna.

"Is your shop busy in the morning?" asks Grace.

"Well, some customers come to our shop in the morning, but most customers come in the afternoon or evening," says Haruna.

"Good!" says Grace. "Now, I am making a movie at the studio near here. I would like you to do my make-up."

Haruna is very surprised. She looks at Grace Lily.

"Pardon? Could you say that again, please?" says Haruna.

"I would like you to do my make-up for the movie," says Grace. "Do you understand?"

"Me? Do your make-up? For a movie?" Haruna says slowly.

"Yes!" says Grace.

"But…but…Ms Lily, I am not a movie make-up artist. I am a cosmetics saleswoman," says Haruna.

"Yes, I know. But I like Nice Ume-leaf Cosmetics. I wear Nice Ume-leaf Cosmetics lipstick, mascara and powder every day. The quality is very high. And I like your technique. You are very professional. You work hard. You listen to me. You answer my questions about cosmetics. You know many things. Your technique is better than my make-up artist's technique. So, I want you to help me," says Grace. "Can you help me? I need your help until December."

"Er…well….I…er…I don't know…er…" says Haruna.

"I need an answer!" says Grace loudly.

"Er…I will talk to my shop staff, and then I will call you," says Haruna quickly.

"OK. Please call my assistant later," says Grace.

Grace, her assistant and bodyguards leave the shop. They get into a large black car and drive away.

A reporter comes into the shop.

"What did Grace ask you? What did she say?" asks the man quickly. Then, a photographer takes Haruna's photograph.

"I'm sorry gentlemen, I can't talk to you now," says Haruna. "Our shop is closed for the next hour."

The men try to ask many questions, but Haruna opens the door and tells them to go outside. She closes the door and locks it.

She goes to the staff room and opens a bottle of cola. She thinks about Grace's request.

It is a good chance to show Nice Ume-leaf Cosmetics to the USA and the world. Many women will watch the movie. She will sell many cosmetics. But she is the shop manager. She must work hard in the shop.

Angela and Emma come into the staff room.

"Haruna, this is a wonderful chance!" says Angela. "You have to say 'yes'!"

"Nice Ume-leaf Cosmetics will be famous around the world!" says Emma.

Haruna feels nervous.

"But I am not a movie make-up artist," says Haruna. "I will make many mistakes."

"Don't worry! You are a cosmetics professional, Haruna! You studied cosmetics and make-up techniques for many years. You will do a great job!" says Angela.

"But I am the manager of this shop. I have to come here every morning," says Haruna.

"Haruna, don't worry! Mornings are not very busy," says Emma. "This is a great chance! Does Takahashi shacho know about this?"

Then, Haruna remembers the phone call from Takahashi shacho. He said, "You must say yes."

"Yes, he does. Now I understand! He called me last night. He said I must say 'yes'. This is it," says Haruna.

"So, call Grace's assistant and say 'yes'!" says Emma.

Haruna calls Grace Lily's assistant.

"I spoke to my staff. I can help Grace. I am very happy to help," says Haruna.

"Good!" says Grace's assistant. "Please come to the studio tomorrow morning at 4:00am."

"4:00am?!" says Haruna. "That is very early!"

"Yes, it is. Make-up and hair styling starts at 4:00am. Please don't be late," says Grace's assistant. "And please bring many cosmetics. The studio manager will talk to the Nice Ume-leaf Cosmetics head office in Tokyo about the money."

CHAPTER TWO

The next morning, Haruna gets up at 3:00am. She is very sleepy. She drinks some coffee. She is hungry, but she is too nervous to eat breakfast. She leaves her apartment. It is dark outside, and the air is cool. She walks to the studio and arrives at 3:55. There is a large gate. Behind the gate, she can see many large buildings. She can see lights and hear many voices.

There is a security guard at the gate.

"Good morning. I am Haruna Yamane from Nice Ume-leaf Cosmetics," says Haruna.

"Good morning Ms Yamane," says the security guard. He opens the gate.

"The studio is in that building over there." He points to a large building. Haruna walks over to the building. There are many people. They are talking loudly. Some people are running. Others are writing on notepads.

Wow, this is a studio. A real movie studio, thinks Haruna.

"Good morning! Are you Haruna?" asks a woman.

Haruna looks at the woman. "Yes, I am," says Haruna.

"I am Jenifer, the head of the make-up department. I will take you to the make-up room. Grace Lily is waiting for you."

Haruna follows Jenifer up some stairs. At the top of the stairs, there is a large door. Jenifer knocks on the door once, and then she and Haruna walk into the room.

There are large mirrors all around the room. There are many tables and boxes of make-up.

"Good morning Haruna!" says Grace Lily. She has no make-up on her face, but her skin is beautiful and smooth.

"Good morning Ms Lily," says Haruna.

"Please call me Grace," says Grace.

"Good morning, Grace," says Haruna. She looks around. *Wow. So much make-up,* she thinks.

Haruna and Jenifer choose some cosmetics. Jenifer gives Haruna instructions about colours and style, and Haruna does Grace's make-up. While she is doing Grace's make-up, no one speaks. The room is very quiet. Haruna concentrates on her job. It takes one hour.

"Have you finished?" asks Grace.

"Yes, I think so," says Haruna.

"Good! Let's go to the studio. The director will be angry if I'm late!" says Grace.

They walk down to the studio together.

Am I dreaming? This cannot be real. I think I'm dreaming, thinks Haruna. *I am a cosmetics saleswoman. Why am I here, walking to a studio with Grace Lily?*

There are many people in the studio – the director, the stage-manager, the assistants and the cameramen. Haruna feels very excited. *I have to email my family and friends! They will be very surprised!* she thinks.

"It's time to start!" shouts the director. "Now! Let's start now!"

Grace and another actor stand on the set. The cameramen stand behind their cameras.

"Action!" shouts the director.

After a few seconds, the director shouts "Stop! Stop! Cut! Cut!"

"Grace, your lips are too red! Where is the make-up artist?"

Everyone looks at Haruna.

"I'm here," says Haruna, quietly.

"Change Grace's lipstick! The lipstick is too red! Change it to pink!" says the director. He looks angry.

Haruna is very nervous. She steps onto the set. The studio lights are very bright and hot. She takes a tissue and some pink lipstick out of her make-up box. Everyone in the studio is watching Haruna. She takes off Grace's lipstick with the tissue and puts on some pink lipstick.

"Okay, let's start again!" says the director.

It is 11:00am. Haruna has to go to the shop. She says goodbye to

Grace and Jenifer.

She walks out of the studio. It is very sunny and hot. She is very hungry. She wants to eat lunch before she goes to the shop.

"Hey, Haruna!"

Haruna turns around.

"David! Hello!" Haruna is very surprised. It is David!

"Guzen!" says David!

"Yes! Guzen! It's a coincidence!" says Haruna. They laugh.

"Do you work here?" asks Haruna.

"Yes, I am a cameraman here," says David. "You did a great job today. Grace loves your cosmetics and she likes you very much."

"Thank you," says Haruna. She is very surprised and happy to see David.

Haruna buys a sandwich for lunch and then goes to the shop. She works at the shop from 12:00pm to 9:00pm. She is very tired, but happy. Many customers come to the shop and she sells many cosmetics. And today, she had a great experience.

CHAPTER THREE

It is December. Every day, Haruna goes to the studio at 4:00am, then, she goes to the shop and works from 12:00pm to 9:00pm. She is very busy every day because many people come to the shop to buy Christmas presents.

Today is Haruna's last day at the studio. Now, Haruna is in the make-up room. She is talking to Grace.

"Grace, how did you know about Nice Ume-leaf Cosmetics? Did you see our shop, or did you see our cosmetics in the newspaper?" asks Haruna.

"A cameraman in the studio bought me some Nice Ume-leaf Cosmetics," says Grace.

"Oh, really? What is his name?" asks Haruna.

"His name is David," says Grace.

"David?" asks Haruna. Then, Haruna remembers…

In October, David came to the cosmetics shop. He bought some cosmetics for his girlfriend. So…Grace is David's girlfriend! Haruna is very shocked.

The next day, when Haruna returns home at night, she sees David in the car park. He is getting out of his car. She walks over to him.

"Hi David," says Haruna.

"Hi Haruna. Are you OK? You look tired," says David.

"I am OK, but I am very tired," says Haruna.

"Are you going back to Japan for New Year?" asks David.

"No, I can't. I have to stay in LA." Haruna is sad. She wants to see her family and she wants to go to Izumo Taisha shrine for hatsumode, the first prayers of the year. And she wants to eat o-sechi ryori, traditional New Year's food. But she must stay in LA. The Christmas and New Year period is very busy.

"I want to see my family and I want to go back to Japan for New Year. I miss my family and friends," says Haruna.

"What are you going to do on December 31st and January 1st?" asks David.

"I don't have any plans. I will stay in my apartment alone," says Haruna. "How about you?"

"Well, my family usually has Christmas dinner together on December 25th. But this year, we are going to have Christmas dinner on December 31st," says David.

"Why? I don't understand," says Haruna.

"My brother has to work at the English school in Izumo on Christmas Day. He cannot come back to the USA for Christmas. He will come back on December 28th. My mother and father want to have Christmas dinner when my brother comes back to LA."

"That's nice," says Haruna. She wants to have dinner with her mother and father and her sister. This is Haruna's second time to spend New Year alone. Last year, she stayed in Tokyo to study for the TOEIC test. This year, she has to work in LA.

"Haruna, please come to my house for dinner on December 31st. You can talk to my brother about Izumo!" says David.

"Really?" asks Haruna. "Thank you, David, you are very kind. But I don't want to be trouble. If I go, your mother and father will have much trouble."

"No! It's no trouble! My mother and father will be very happy to meet you! When my brother first went to Izumo, he couldn't speak Japanese. He had much trouble. But many Japanese people helped him. Japanese people are very kind to my brother. So, I want to be kind to you," says David. "I want to help you, and I want you to come for dinner! It will be fun! So, what do you think?"

Haruna smiles at David. "OK! Thank you! I accept your offer!"

CHAPTER FOUR

It is December 31st. Haruna is at David's house. It is a very big house with an outdoor swimming pool and a large garden. Haruna, David, his mother, father and brother are sitting in the dining room. They are eating. There is a lot of food – potatoes, turkey, vegetables, cake, and ice-cream, and there are many bottles of wine and beer. David's mother and father are very kind. His brother, Peter, is very interesting. Haruna and Peter are talking about Shimane.

"Which places do you like best in Shimane, Peter?" asks Haruna.

"I like Izumo Taisha shrine and Matsue Castle," says Peter.

"My house is near Matsue Castle," says Haruna. "I will take you to my house for dinner someday."

"Thank you," says Peter. "My girlfriend is from Matsue, too."

"Oh really?" says Haruna.

"*Guzen!* It's a coincidence!" says David.

Everyone laughs.

Haruna looks at David. *Where is Grace? Grace is David's girlfriend, but she is not here at the dinner party. Why not? It's strange,* she thinks.

"David, where is Grace?" asks Haruna.

"Grace? I don't know," says David.

"Will she come later?" asks Haruna.

"Of course not! Why? I don't understand," says David.

"Is Grace your girlfriend?" asks Haruna.

"No! She isn't my girlfriend! Why do you think so?" asks David.

"Really? She isn't your girlfriend?" asks Haruna. She is very surprised.

"Really! She is not my girlfriend," says David. "Why do you think she is my girlfriend?"

"Because you came to my shop in October. You bought Nice Ume-leaf Cosmetics for your girlfriend. Grace said you bought cosmetics for her. So, I think Grace is your girlfriend," says Haruna.

David laughs. "No, Haruna! You made a mistake! In October, I told all my friends and co-workers about your shop. I gave everyone the pamphlets and free samples. Grace and Jenifer like to try new cosmetics so I went to your shop to buy some cosmetics for Grace."

"But in the shop, you said, 'I would like to buy some cosmetics for my girlfriend.' I don't understand," says Haruna.

"Yes, that's right. I couldn't say 'I'd like to buy some cosmetics for Grace Lily.' That is private information," says David. "Grace is a very famous person. It was a secret."

"I see!" says Haruna. "I'm sorry David. I misunderstood."

"No problem!" says David. "Here, have some more wine!"

Haruna feels very happy. Grace is not David's girlfriend!

It is 11:59pm. Haruna and David's family are drinking expensive champagne in the living room.

"I hope we all have a wonderful year!" says David. Everyone starts the countdown.

"Ten! Nine! Eight! Seven! Six! Five! Four! Three! Two! One! Happy New Year!"

Haruna drinks her champagne. She thinks about the past year. She took the TOEIC test, got a high score, came to LA, worked in the cosmetics shop, sold many cosmetics, met Grace Lily, worked in a movie studio, and met David. What a wonderful year!

"Haruna, are you OK?" asks David.

"Yes, I am. Thank you. I am thinking about my life. I am very happy here in LA. I had a good year. But I am also a little sad."

"Why are you sad?" asks David.

"Because I like LA, and I want to stay here. But, I like Japan too, and I want to see my family and friends," says Haruna.

"Can you take a vacation next year?" asks David.

"I don't know. My boss, Takahashi shacho, is not very kind," says Haruna.

"Every day he says 'Yamane san! Work harder! Work harder!' So, maybe I can't take a vacation."

"But you did a great job! Nice Ume-leaf Cosmetics is very famous in the USA now. You are a great worker, Haruna. I think Mr Takahashi is very happy."

"No…Takahashi shacho is never happy. He is always angry," says Haruna.

"Don't worry Haruna! It's New Year! This year will be great! Let's drink some more champagne!" says David.

Haruna smiles. David is always happy and he is very kind. She likes him very much. Does he like Haruna too?

CHAPTER FIVE

It is the end of January. Haruna is in the shop. The phone rings.

"Hello, Nice Ume-leaf Cosmetics, LA Shop, Haruna Yamane speaking," says Haruna.

"Hello Haruna! It's Jenifer, Grace Lily's make-up artist."

"Hello Jenifer! How are you?"

"I'm good thanks, how are you?"

"I'm fine, thanks."

"Haruna, I have some very big, important news!" says Jenifer. "Grace Lily has been nominated for an Academy Award. She might win an Oscar!"

"Really? An Academy Award?" asks Haruna. "Wow! That's fantastic!"

"Yes! It's great news! So, Grace Lily will go to the Academy Awards ceremony in Hollywood," says Jenifer.

"Wonderful! I will watch it on TV!" says Haruna.

"No, Haruna. You will not watch it on TV. You will come to the ceremony too," says Jenifer.

"Pardon? I don't understand," says Haruna. "I will….what?"

"Grace Lily wants to wear make-up from Nice Ume-leaf Cosmetics at the ceremony. She wants you to do her make-up before the ceremony," says Jenifer.

"Really? Me? She wants me to go to the ceremony?" asks Haruna.

"Yes. The ceremony is a very big event. It is the biggest night of the year for Grace. It is the biggest event in Grace's career! It is really important! Can you do it?" asks Jenifer.

"Er…well….er….I don't know. I will call my boss in Tokyo and ask him," says Haruna.

"Also, after the ceremony, there is a big party. Many famous movie stars will go to the party. Grace Lily will give you a ticket for the party," says Jenifer.

"The Academy Award party? Me!? But I am not famous!" says Haruna.

"It's OK. Many workers from the movie studios go to the party. I will go to the party, too. Grace wants us to check her make-up at the party," says Jenifer.

"But I don't have a dress," says Haruna.

"Don't worry," says Jenifer. "The studio will lend you a beautiful dress!"

"Really? Oh, OK…and…er…will David go to the party too?" asks Haruna.

"Yes, I think so," says Jenifer.

"I'll call you back in a few minutes Jenifer," says Haruna.

Haruna thinks carefully about the Academy Award ceremony and party. Then, she has an idea.

Haruna calls Takahashi shacho. She tells him the news. They talk about Haruna's idea. Then, she calls Jenifer.

"Hello, Jenifer. It's Haruna. I talked to my boss. I can do Grace Lily's make up for the ceremony, but we want to ask a favour," says Haruna.

"A favour? What kind of favour?" asks Jenifer.

"At the ceremony, many TV announcers and newspaper reporters will interview Grace Lily. They will ask Grace many questions about her dress, her shoes and her cosmetics. I want Grace to tell the newspaper reporters and TV announcers about Nice Ume-leaf Cosmetics," says Haruna. "She must say to the TV announcers 'My makeup is from Nice Ume-leaf Cosmetics'. Is that okay? Can she do that?"

"I think so. I'm sure Grace can do that," says Jenifer.

Haruna is very happy. She had a very good idea. This is a great chance to tell the world about Nice Ume-leaf Cosmetics and to make her shop very famous!

CHAPTER SIX

It is the day of the Academy Award ceremony. Haruna goes to Grace Lily's hotel room and does Grace's make up. Grace Lily is wearing a long silver dress. She looks beautiful. Then, Haruna gets changed. The studio has lent Haruna a long black dress. She puts the dress on and looks in the mirror. She looks like a movie star.

This is a dream. I must be dreaming, she thinks.

Grace Lily goes to the theatre in a large car. Haruna, Jenifer and other assistants go in a smaller car. They arrive at the theatre. Haruna looks out of the window. There are so many people!

Haruna and Jenifer go to the staff area of the theatre.

Grace Lily is on the red carpet. Many photographers are taking her photograph.

Haruna has many cosmetics samples in her bag.

Last week, Takahashi shacho said, "Take some free samples to the party! Give the samples to the movie stars!"

Haruna is very nervous. She is too shy to talk to movie stars. Also, there are many bodyguards, security guards and assistants.

She sits in the staff area, and does not speak to anyone.

The ceremony starts. Haruna and Jenifer sit backstage. They cannot see the stage. They cannot see anything! Haruna watches the ceremony on her mobile phone and checks the information on Twitter.

Haruna looks at the time. It is nearly the time for the Best Actress award. Will Grace Lily win an Oscar? Haruna hopes so.

Then, they hear the announcement on the speaker.

"This is it, Haruna! Let's listen!" says Jenifer.

They hear the announcement: "And the winner of the Best Actress Award is…Grace Lily!"

"It's Grace! It's Grace! She won!" shouts Jenifer.

Jenifer and Haruna stand up and hug each other. They are very happy. Grace is the winner!

Jenifer and Haruna go to the party after the ceremony. They stand in the corner, watching the famous movie stars.

This is amazing. I'm so lucky, thinks Haruna. She looks across the room and sees Grace Lily. A newspaper reporter is interviewing her.

"Who designed your dress Grace?" asks the newspaper reporter.

"It is a Gucci dress," says Grace.

"Who designed your shoes?"

"Christian Louboutin."

"What make-up are you wearing?"

"I'm wearing Nice Ume-leaf Cosmetics. It is a Japanese brand," says Grace. She looks around the room. Then, she sees Haruna.

"Haruna! Haruna! Come here!" shouts Grace Lily.

Haruna walks over to Grace Lily.

"This is Haruna. She is from Nice Ume-leaf Cosmetics. She did my make-up," says Grace.

Haruna smiles. Many photographers take her photograph. There are some TV cameramen filming her, too.

Later, Haruna feels tired. She sits down in the corner.

"Hey, Haruna! Are you okay?"

"David! Hi! Yes, I'm fine, but I feel tired. My life is like a dream!" says Haruna.

"I'm a cosmetics saleswoman from Matsue, a small city in Japan. Why am I here, at the Academy Award party? I don't understand. It must be a dream!"

"Haruna, you are here because you work hard, and because your company makes very good cosmetics. Also, you are here because Grace Lily likes you very much," says David.

"But, Grace Lily is a famous movie star. Why does she like me?" asks Haruna.

"Haruna, movies stars are human beings. They are normal people. They need friends, too. And the movie business is a business. Money is very important. So, studios need good cosmetics, good make-up artists, good fashion designers and good cameramen. It is business. It is not special," says David.

"I see," says Haruna. "But it is special to me."

"Haruna, you are special," says David.

Haruna looks at David.

"Pardon?" asks Haruna. *What did he say?*

David smiles and sits down next to her.

"You are special Haruna," says David. "Haruna…I like…"

Then, Haruna's phone rings. Bad timing!

"Sorry David, please excuse me," she says.

She answers the phone. "Hello?"

"Yamane san. It's Takahashi."

"Oh, hello Takahashi shacho."

"Yamane san. Did you give the movie stars the cosmetics samples?" asks Takahashi shacho.

"No, I didn't," says Haruna.

"Why not? Give the samples to the movie stars, now!" says Takahashi shacho.

"But, Takahashi shacho, the movie stars are very busy! They are talking and eating, and…"

Takahashi shacho is angry. "Give them the samples! Now!"

Haruna says goodbye and hangs up the phone.

"I'm sorry, David. I have to give samples to movie stars," says Haruna.

"Good luck!" says David. "Let's talk tomorrow."

Haruna tries to give some samples to movie stars, but they are very busy. Some are kind, but some are not friendly. She goes home. She thinks about David. At the party he said "Haruna, you are special…I like…."

What does he like? Who does he like? Does he like me? thinks Haruna. She tries to sleep, but she cannot. She thinks about the ceremony and about David all night. She falls asleep at 4:00am.

CHAPTER SEVEN

Haruna wakes up. Her phone is ringing. She looks at the clock. It is 5:00am.

She answers the phone.

"Hello?"

"Hello! It's Takahashi."

"Takahashi shacho, good morning…er, sorry, good evening," says Haruna. Takahashi shacho always calls her when she is sleeping. He never thinks about the time difference. He only thinks about the company.

"Yamane san, you are on NHK news!" says Takahashi shacho.

"Pardon?"

"You are on NHK news with Grace Lily! At the party, the reporter asked Grace Lily, 'What make-up are you wearing?' Grace Lily said, 'I'm wearing Nice Ume-leaf Cosmetics. This is Haruna. She is from Nice Ume-leaf Cosmetics. She did my make-up.' Yamane san, the interview is on TV on NHK news and CNN! Nice Ume-leaf Cosmetics is very famous! You had a great idea Yamane san. A great idea!" says Takahashi shacho.

Haruna feels good. She gets up and eats a slice of toast and drinks two cups of coffee for breakfast. She has only slept for one hour so she feels very sleepy.

At 8:00am she goes to the shop. Today many customers will come to the shop, so she opens early, at 8:30am.

Many customers come to the shop and buy many cosmetics. Many newspaper reporters also come to the shop. They ask Haruna about

Nice Ume-leaf Cosmetics and Grace Lily. Some photographers take photographs of the cosmetics display counter and of Haruna, Emma and Angela.

At 12:30, the phone rings.

"Hello, Nice Ume-leaf Cosmetics, LA Shop, Haruna Yamane speaking," says Haruna.

"Hello. It's Matsumoto."

"Hello Matsumoto san," says Haruna. "How is the New York shop?"

"It is very good. Today, many customers are in my shop. Everyone watched the interview with Grace Lily on TV. They want to buy Nice Ume-leaf Cosmetics," says Kana.

"Good! I'm very happy!" says Haruna.

"Yamane san, thank you very much. In Tokyo, you were my rival. But, now, you helped me. You work hard in LA, and you made Nice Ume-leaf Cosmetics very famous in the USA. Thank you Yamane san. You helped me a lot. Thanks to you, my shop is very busy," says Kana.

"You helped me too, Matsumoto san," says Haruna. "You were my rival. So, I tried my best. Thanks to you, I did a good job."

"Yamane san, I have a vacation next month," says Kana. "Can I come to LA to see you?"

"Of course! Let's go to Universal Studios Hollywood together!" says Haruna.

"That is a great idea!" says Kana. "See you then!"

Haruna is happy and surprised. Haruna and Kana will become friends!

CHAPTER EIGHT

It is March. December, January and February were very busy months. But next month, Haruna will go back to Japan. A new manager will come to the LA shop. Haruna is a little sad, but also a little happy. She wants to stay in LA, because she likes David and she likes the shop. But she wants to see her family and friends in Japan, too.

The phone rings.

"Hello, Nice Ume-leaf Cosmetics, LA Shop, Haruna Yamane speaking," says Haruna.

"It's Takahashi."

"Hello Takahashi shacho," says Haruna.

"Yamane san, I have a new plan," says Takahashi shacho. "I will open thirty shops in the USA this year."

"Thirty shops? Really? That is wonderful!" says Haruna.

"Yes, it is. Yamane san, do you want to stay in the USA?" asks Takahashi shacho.

"Yes, I do. But I want to see my family and friends in Japan, too," says Haruna.

"Yamane san. I had a meeting with the company directors. We want you to stay in the USA. You did a very good job in LA. You have many good ideas," says Takahashi shacho.

"Oh, thank you," says Haruna.

"We want you to be the USA director," says Takahashi shacho.

"USA director? Me? A director?" asks Haruna. She is very shocked.

"Yes, a director. The top manager in the USA!" says Takahashi shacho.

"I don't know. It is a very difficult job," says Haruna. "Can I think about it?"

"You don't need to think about it! It is the perfect job for you! You can stay in LA, you can get a higher salary and you can have three long vacations. You can come to Japan at New Year, and in May for the Golden Week holiday. And you can have a long summer holiday too," says Takahashi shacho. "Say 'yes', Yamane san!"

Haruna smiles. Tears start to fall down her face. "Okay. Yes! Yes! Thank you! I will do my best!" she says.

"Thank you, Yamane san. You are a great worker!" says Takahashi shacho.

Haruna sits down in the staff room and cries.

Me! Director! I can't believe it! she thinks. *I can't believe it!*

Haruna goes home at 9:00pm. She sees David on the apartment block stairs.

"Hi David! How are you?"

"Hey Haruna! I'm good thanks, how are you?"

"I'm very happy!" says Haruna.

"Really? Why?"

"I had some good news today. Takahashi shacho called me. From April, I am the USA director of Nice Ume-leaf Cosmetics!" says Haruna.

"Really? Wow! That's great! Congratulations!" says David.

"Thank you!" says Haruna.

"Haruna, let's celebrate!" says David.

"Celebrate? How?" asks Haruna.

"Let's go for dinner together!" says David. "Are you free on Sunday night?"

"Sunday night? Yes, I am free. I don't have any plans," says Haruna.

"Great! Let's go to the new French restaurant near the studio. Is 7:00pm OK?"

"Yes, 7:00pm is fine. Thank you David! See you then!" says Haruna.

Haruna is excited. She has a date with David on Sunday night!

CHAPTER NINE

It is Sunday night.

Haruna and David are in the restaurant. It is a very expensive restaurant. Haruna is wearing a blue dress. David is wearing a suit. The food is delicious. They drink champagne and talk about many things.

"Haruna, Peter asked me to visit him in Izumo. When is the best season to visit?" asks David.

"I think May is best," says Haruna. "In June it rains a lot, and it is very hot and humid in July and August."

"May? OK, I will talk to Peter about it," says David.

"I am going to visit my family in Matsue in the first week of May," says Haruna. "It is Golden Week."

"Oh really?" asks David.

"Yes," says Haruna. She looks at David. Then she has a good idea. "David, we can go together!"

"Really? That would be great! Thank you Haruna!" says David.

"You are welcome," says Haruna. "I will take you and Peter to many places in Matsue. We will have a very good time."

"Excellent! I will call Peter tomorrow. He will be very happy. You are very kind, Haruna. Thank you."

"You're welcome." Haruna smiles at David. "We have to go to Izumo Taisha shrine, too. It is famous for *go-en*. Now, I believe in *go-en*!"

"Pardon? What is *go-en*?" asks David.

"*Go-en* is a Japanese word. In English it is…" Haruna thinks. She doesn't know how to say 'go-en' in English.

"I don't know the English, but I can give you an example," says Haruna. "For example, I met Julie in Tokyo. Julie is American. She likes Nice Ume-leaf Cosmetics. She went to the shop in Ginza and she told the shop staff that her friends in LA like Nice Ume-leaf Cosmetics. So, Takahashi shacho decided to open an LA shop, and I could come to LA. Then, I met you. You live in my apartment building, and you work in a studio, and..."

"So, *go-en* is like *guzen*? A coincidence?" asks David.

"No...it is different...So, I met you and you work in a movie studio. You gave Grace Lily the Nice Ume-leaf Cosmetics samples. Then, I met Grace Lily. Grace liked me and Nice Ume-leaf Cosmetics, and then I went to the Academy Award party. Then, my shop became very famous. And, your brother Peter lives in Izumo. Izumo is near my hometown. Izumo is famous for 'go-en'. Maybe my friends and family think 'Haruna is lucky'. But, I don't think I am lucky. I think it is the special power of 'go-en'" says Haruna.

"Special power?" says David. "Is *go-en* a kind of fate?"

"Fate? I don't know that word," says Haruna.

"Fate. Like destiny, or fortune," says David.

"Destiny...yes, maybe something like that!" says Haruna. "Izumo Taisha shrine is very famous for that special power. It is the power of special connections."

"Well, you can teach me about *go-en* when we go to Izumo!" says David.

"Yes! I will!" says Haruna.

The waiter pours some champagne into their glasses.

David and Haruna lift their glasses.

"Cheers!" They drink the champagne and smile at each other.

In May, Haruna and David will go to Japan together. She feels very, very happy!

THANK YOU

Thank you for reading Haruna's Story Part 3! We hope you enjoyed the story. (Word count: 5,585)

There are quizzes about this book on our free study site I Talk You Talk Press EXTRA. http://italk-youtalk.com

If you would like to read more graded readers, please visit our website
http://www.italkyoutalk.com

Other Level 1 graded readers include
A Business Trip to New York
A Homestay in Auckland
A Trip to London
Dear Ellen
Haruna's Story Part 1
Haruna's Story Part 2
Ken's Story Part 1
Ken's Story Part 2
Life is Surprising!
Strange Stories
The Christmas Present
The Old Hospital
We Met Online

ABOUT THE AUTHOR

I Talk You Talk Press is a Japan-based publisher of language textbooks, graded readers and language learning/teaching resources.

Our team is made up of highly experienced language teachers and translators, who have all studied at least one additional language to an advanced level.

This experience enables us to design our materials from the perspective of both the teacher and the learner. We consult with both teachers and language learners when designing our textbooks and graded readers, and test our materials extensively in the classroom before publication.

We are a fast-growing press, and currently publish graded readers for learners of English. We publish new graded readers monthly.

www.ingramcontent.com/pod-product-compliance
Lightning Source LLC
Chambersburg PA
CBHW022352040426
42449CB00006B/835